it is all
about the
bulge

sexy

//

adjective

1. 1.

sexually attractive or exciting.

"sexy French underwear"

synonyms:

sexually attractive, seductive, desirable, alluring, inviting, sensual, sultry, slinky, provocative, tempting, tantalizing; More

-

1. 2.

INFORMAL

very exciting or appealing.

"business magazines might not seem like the sexiest career choice"

synonyms:

exciting, stimulating, interesting, appealing, intriguing;

GYM

GYM

GYM

REW CHRISTIAN

TROPHY BOY

HY BOY

PALM
TROPHY BOY

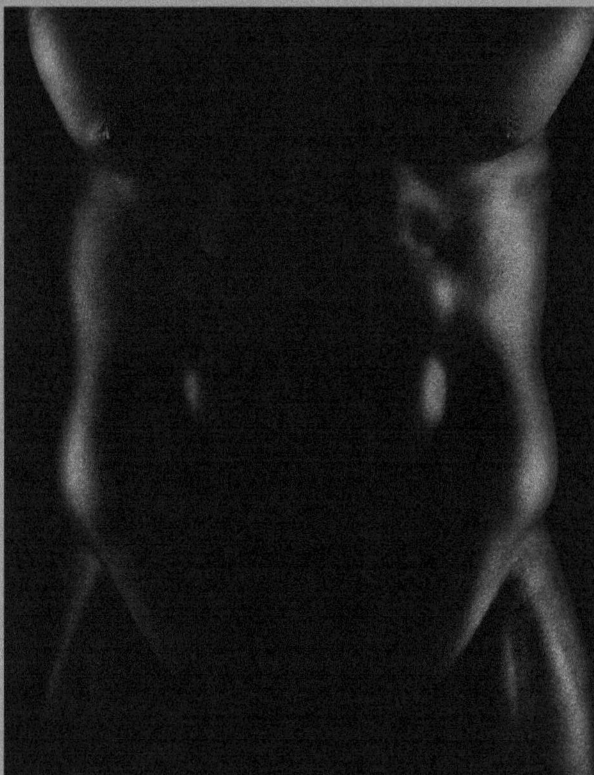

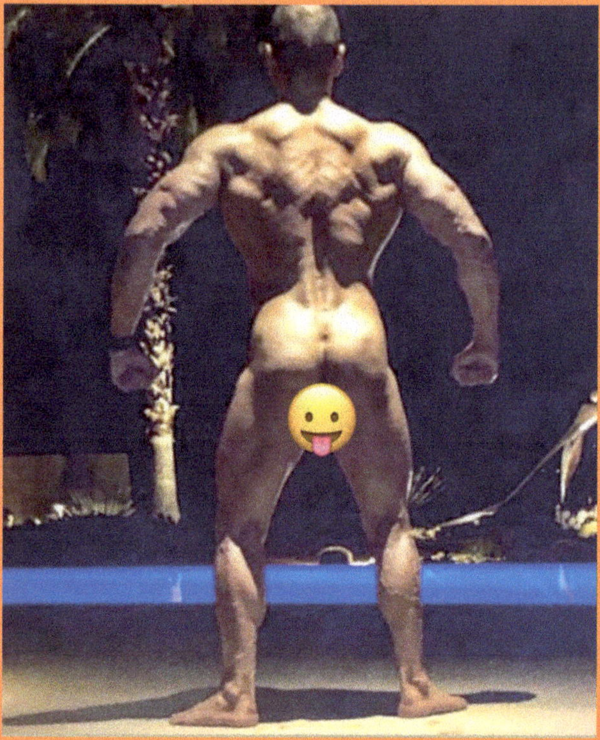

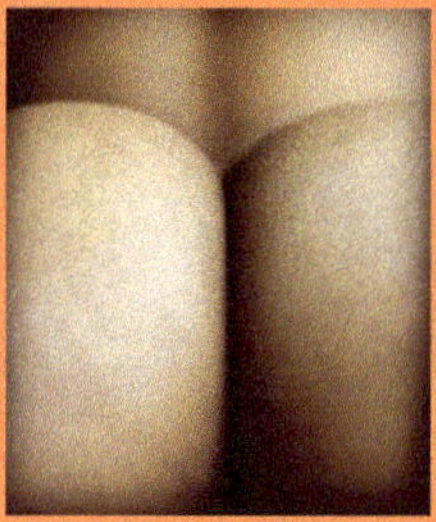

MARTIN RANCHO MIRAGE
TROPHY BOY

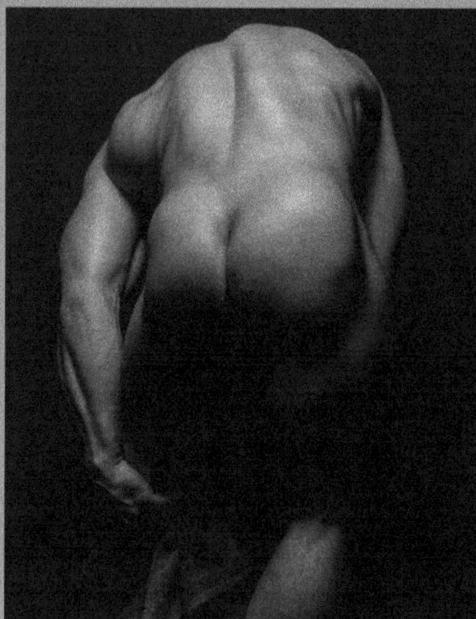

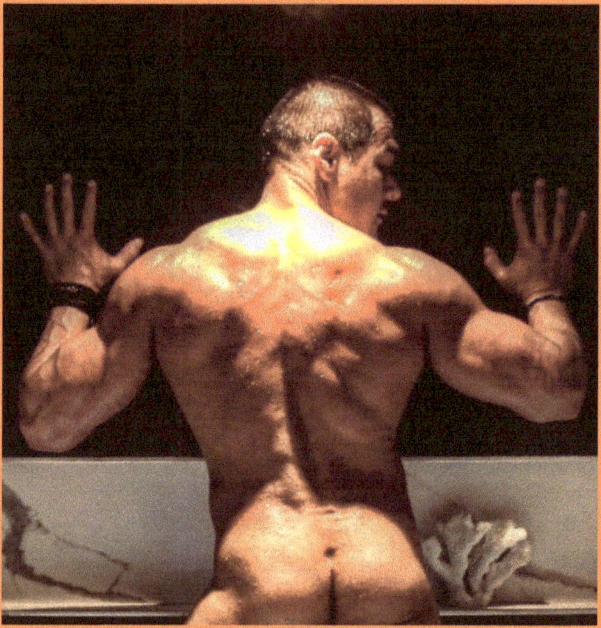

1577

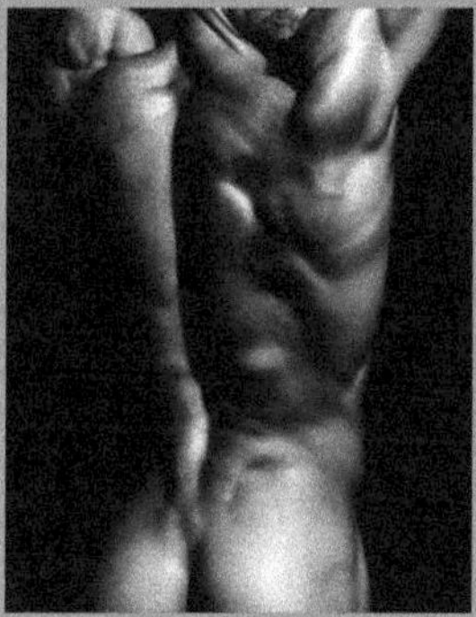

BOY

TROPHY BO

NASTYPIG

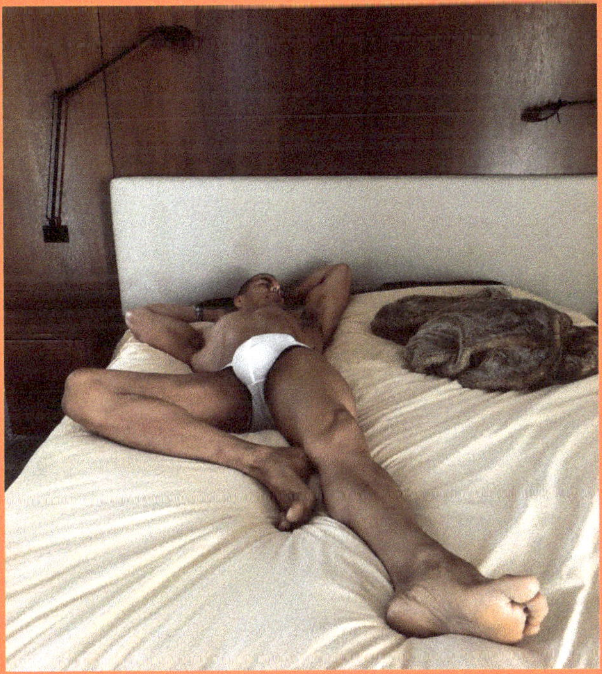

Charles Moniz Photography

Charles Moniz Photography

Charles Moniz Photography

STOP
ROAD
CLOSED

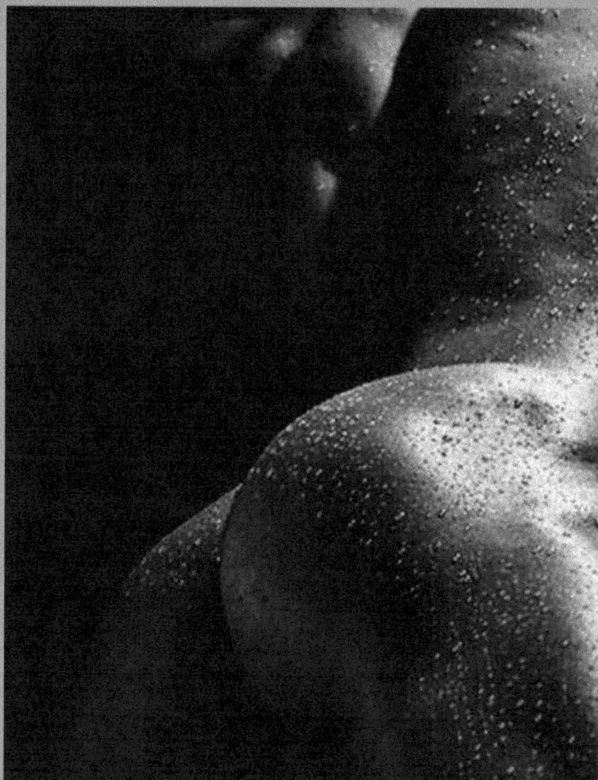

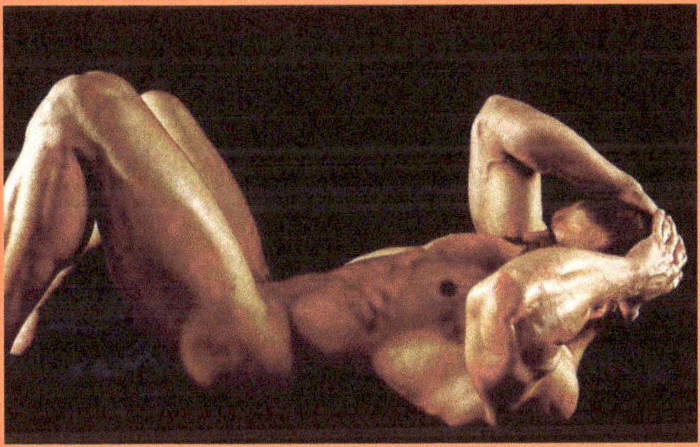

WPPV

TROPHY BOY

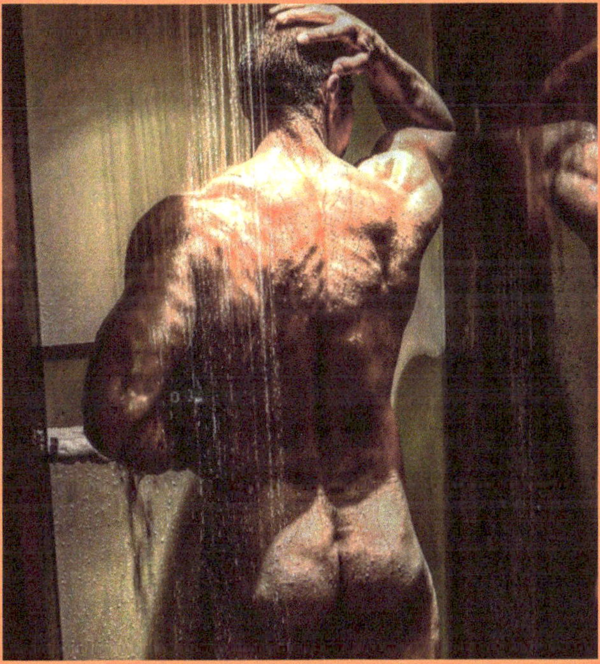

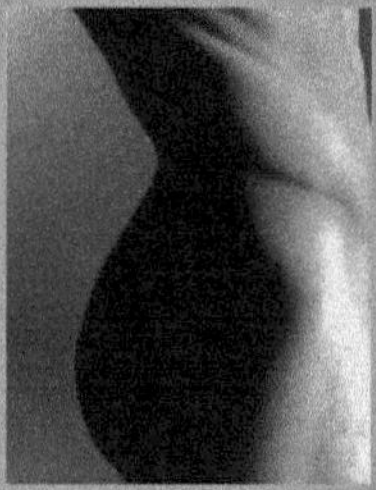

2

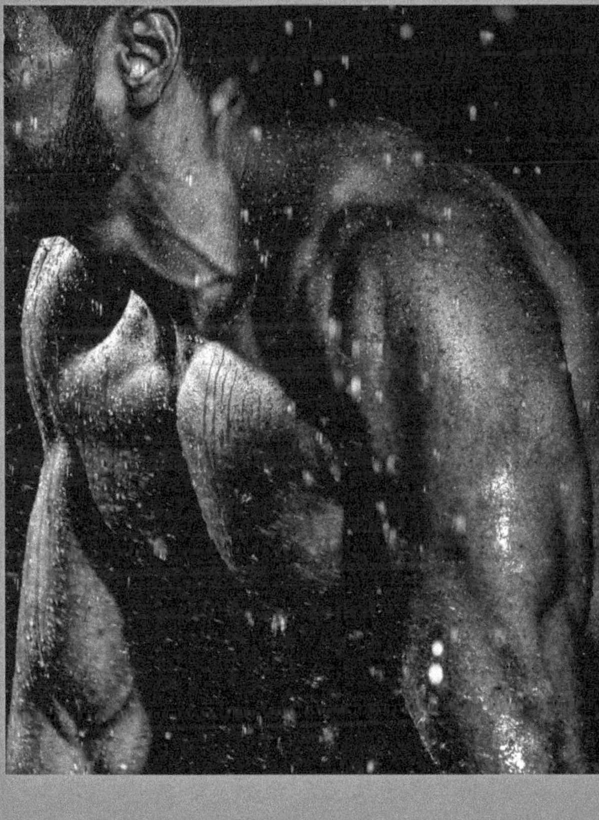

CHADA THAI

ANDREW CHRISTIAN
TROPHY BOY
2019 CALENDAR

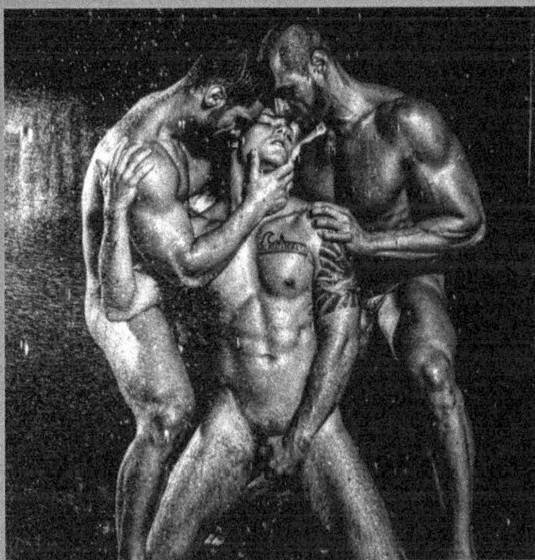

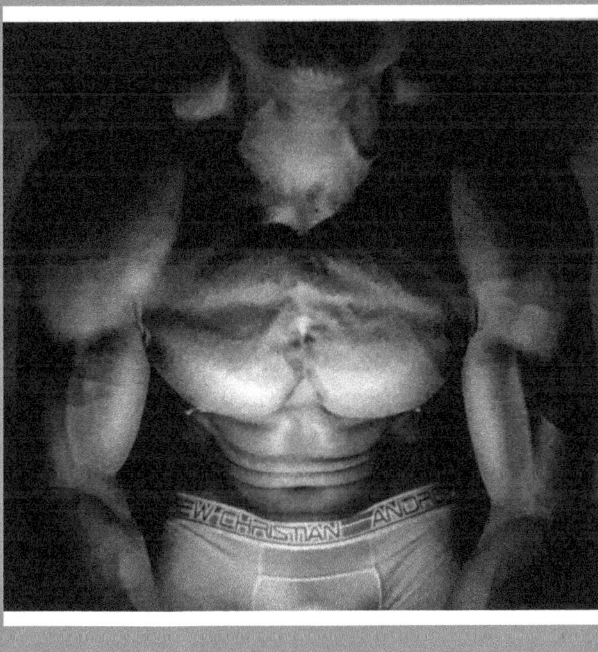
CHRISTIAN

JUAN FRANCISCO

NORWEGIAN PEARL

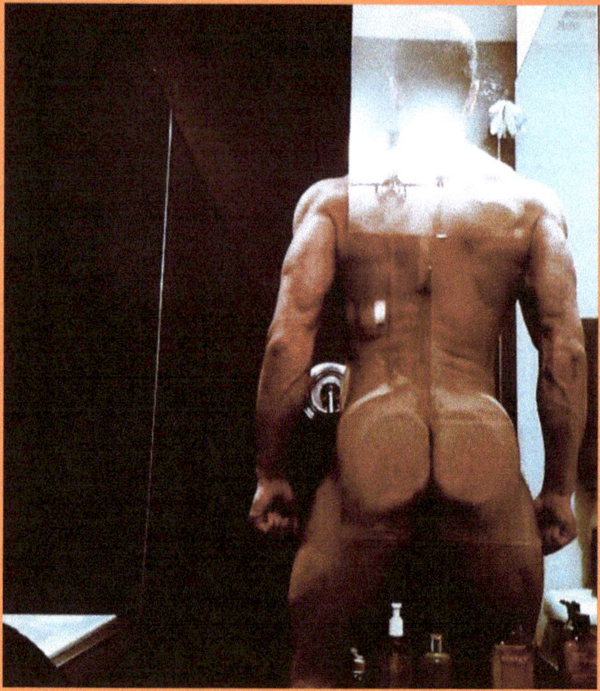

Porto

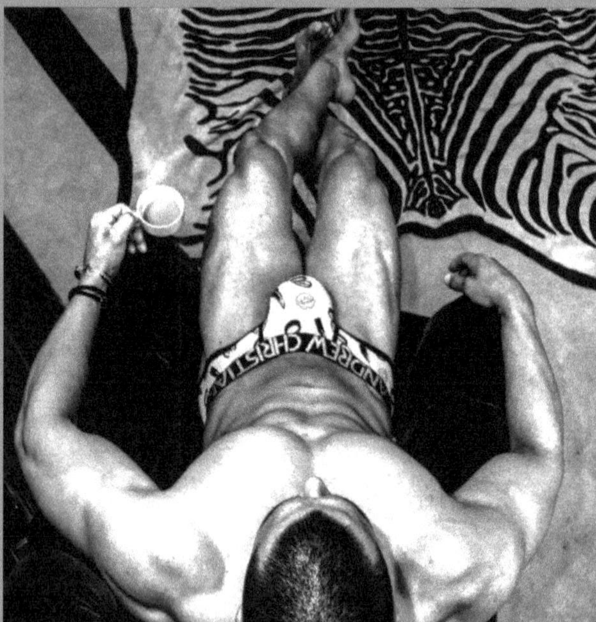

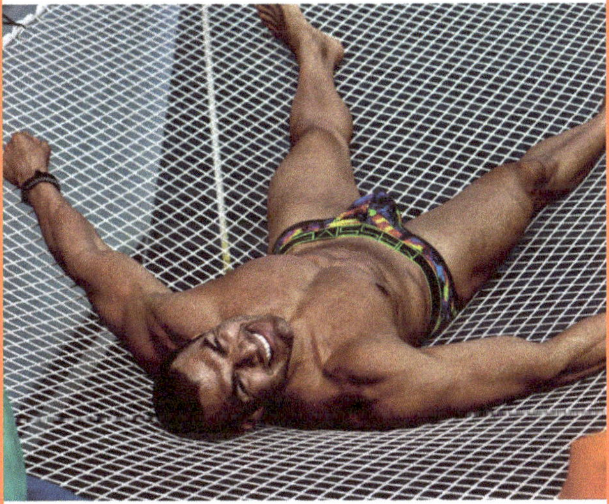

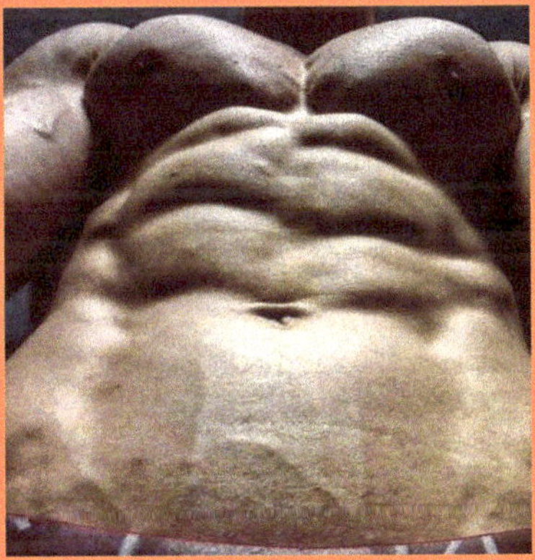

TROPHY

TEAM NO LIMITS
BULK

ANDREW

TROPHY

MASSIVE

FESTIVAL OF
ARTS

TROPHY BOY

TROPHY BOY

TROPHY

WORLD GYM
WORLD GYM

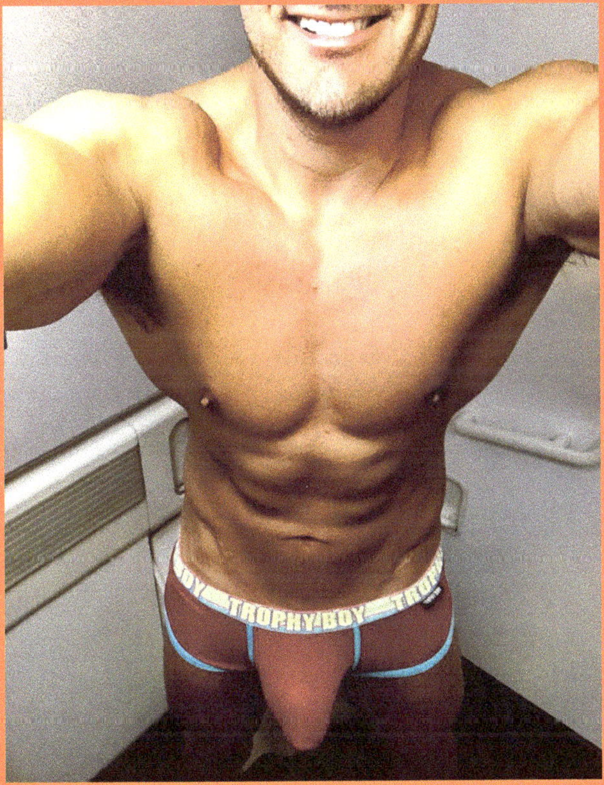
TROPHY BOY

ANDREW

ANDREW

MENU
INFO.
START/
STOP
1/250
11
100-9102
50/81

BARCELONA

THE PIANO
MASSIVE

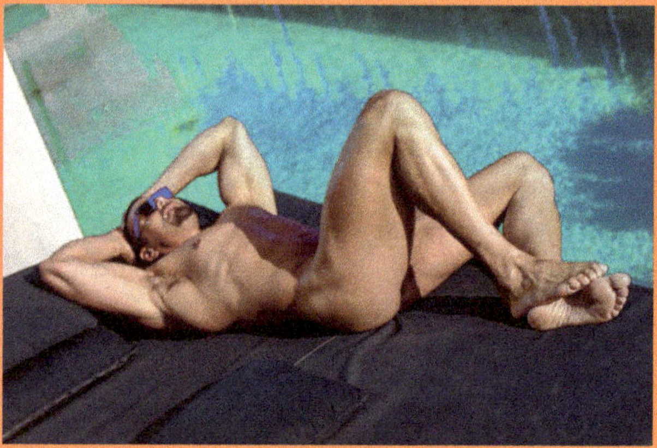

TROPHY

GAME OF
THRONES
WHITE PARTY

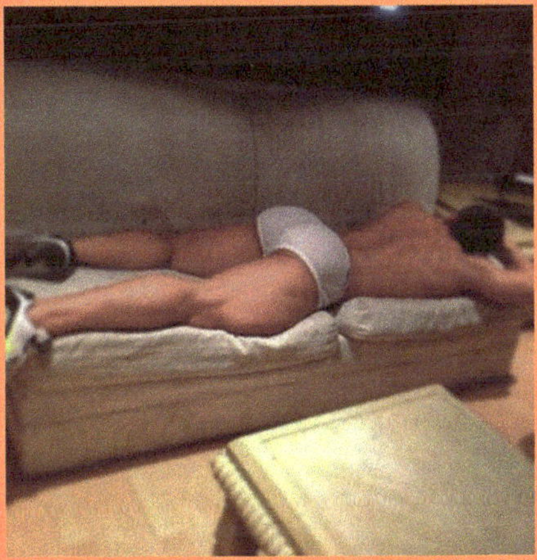

Forbes
Forbes

JAN
CALIFORNIA
1DRFULL

STYLE
LULU

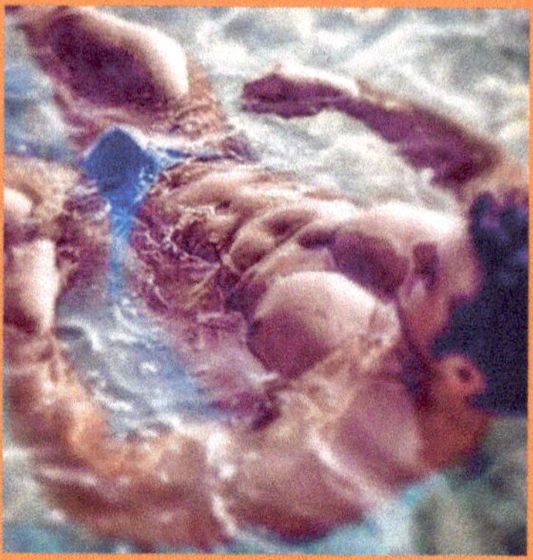

LANGLEY CITY
FIRE DEPT.

190

NO LIMITS

ASTON MARTIN

CPSIA information can be obtained
at www.ICGtesting.com
Printed in the USA
BVHW091003010419
544231BV00024B/1861/P

9 780368 481765